Animal Magic

Essential daily exercises for the young pianist

by
Fanny Waterman

FABER **ff** MUSIC

To the Pupil

Do you want to become a fine pianist? If so, you need to develop an excellent technique so that you can support your musical ideas by playing all the notes beautifully.

Practise the exercises in **Animal Magic** every day – they will only take about 10 minutes altogether. Play each one several times, loudly and slowly at first, then gradually increase the speed as you gain more confidence. Play with bent fingers, lifting them as high as possible with a perfect see-saw movement between them. Try not to overlap any notes, and keep a steady beat.

If you practise the exercises every day, you will soon notice a great improvement in your playing!

To the Teacher

These essential warming up exercises represent a distillation of those by Czerny, Philipp, Hanon and Dohnanyi, and require your constant supervision for maximum benefit. Exercises Nos. **1–9** are specifically designed for finger-strengthening, while Nos. **10–26** develop various other aspects of technique. They should form an essential part of your pupil's daily practice routine.

Fanny Waterman

© Faber Music Ltd 1990
First published in 1990 by Faber Music Ltd,
3 Queen Square London WC1N 3AU

Music drawn by Sheila Stanton
Designed and illustrated by Julia Osorno
Cover typography by Julia Osorno

Typeset by Bookworm Typesetting, Manchester
Printed in England
International copyright secured
All rights reserved

Climb like a spider

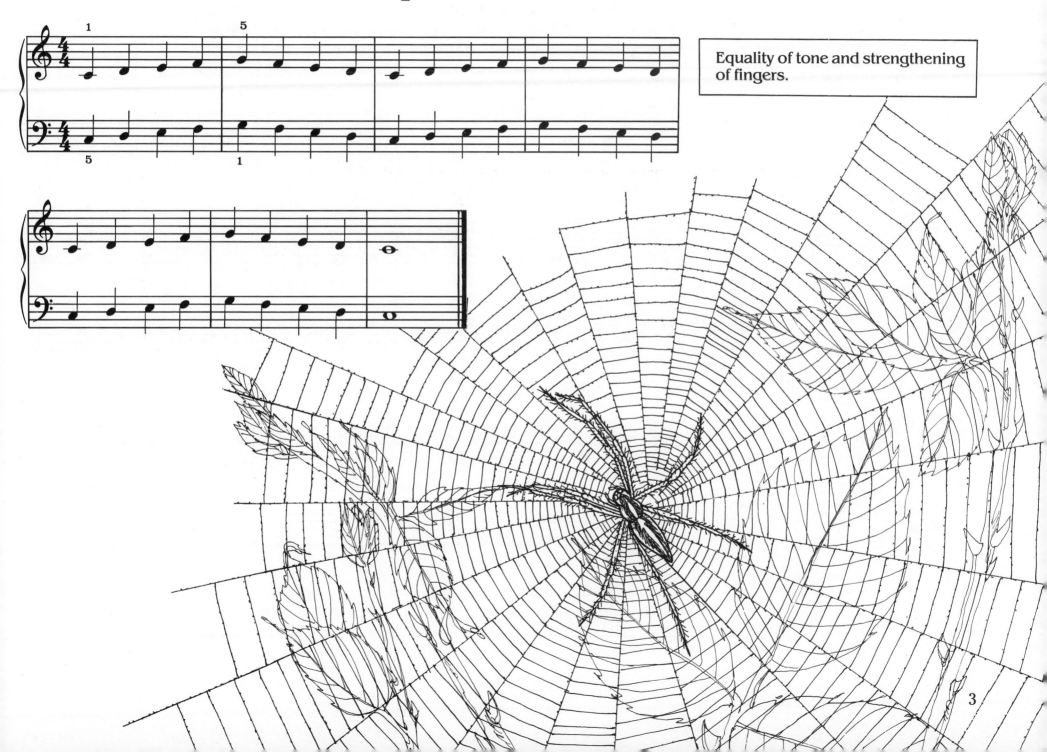

Equality of tone and strengthening of fingers.

Crawl like a worm

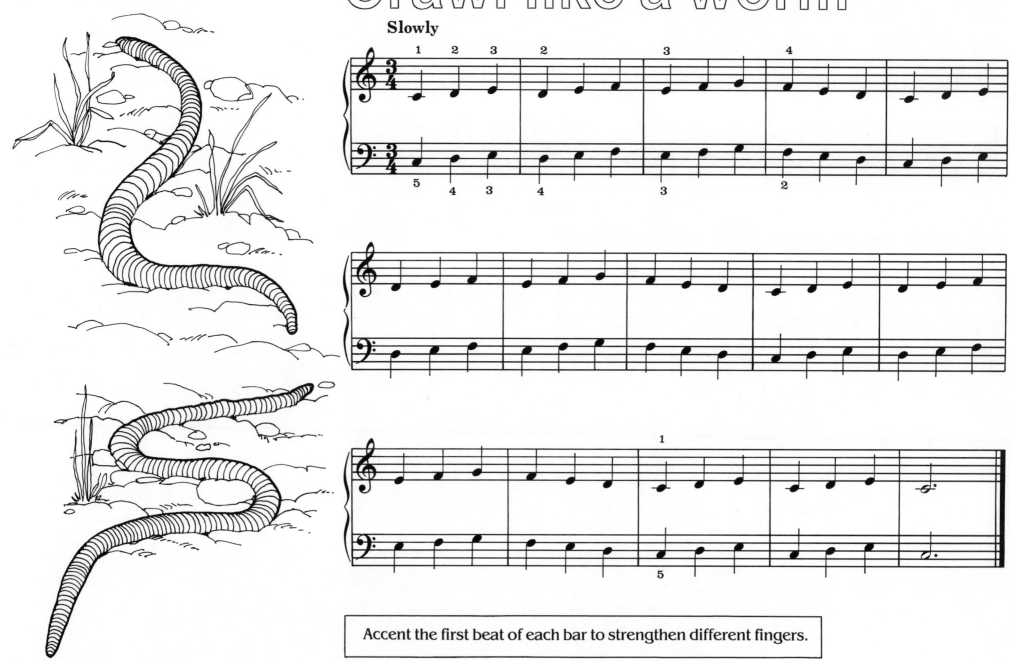

Accent the first beat of each bar to strengthen different fingers.

Cling like a caterpillar

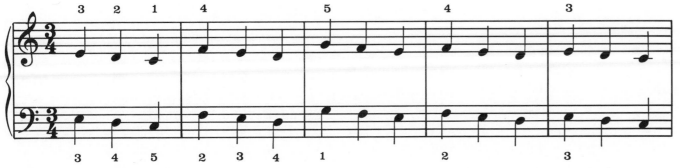

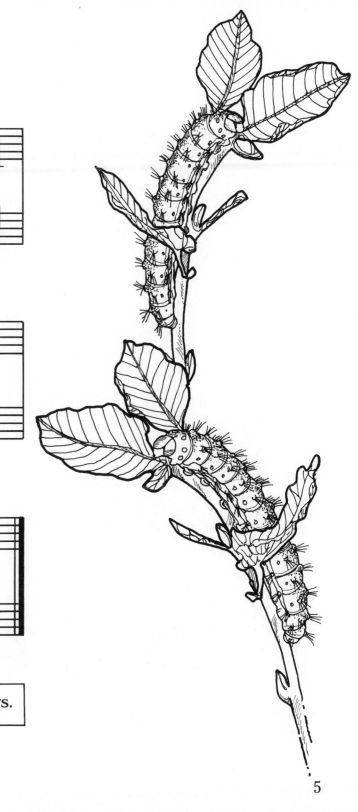

Another pattern to strengthen the fingers.

5

Slither like a snake

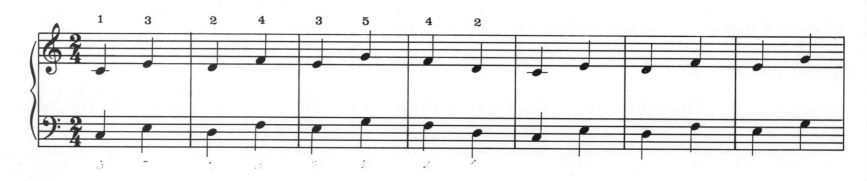

Transfer the weight from one finger to another.

Walk like a racehorse

Play slowly and steadily.

Trot like a racehorse

Equality of fingers on each quaver at a moderate speed.

Canter like a racehorse

Tight rhythm and smart accents — for the RH third finger and LH thumb.
Play hands separately at first, then together.

Gallop like a racehorse

Tight rhythm, smart accents.

Gallop like the winning racehorse!

Get your fingers moving towards the thumb.

Cluck like a chicken

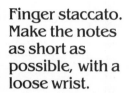

Finger staccato.
Make the notes
as short as
possible, with a
loose wrist.

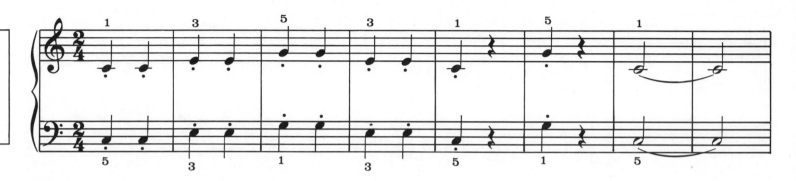

10

Peck like a woodpecker

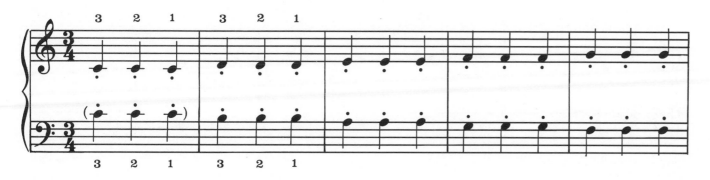

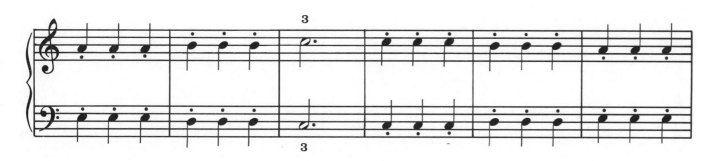

Match up the length of the staccato notes. Play very slowly, hands separately at first.

Spring like a spaniel

Drop on to the first note with a
loose wrist and spring up lightly
on the second.

Use wrist

14/7

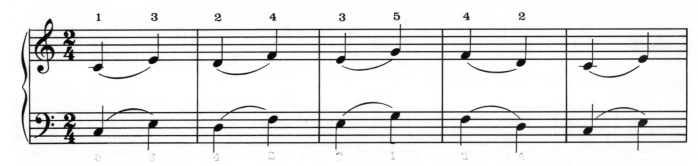

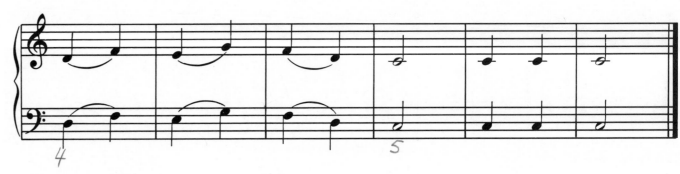

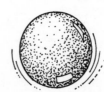

12

Swing like a monkey

Loose wrist; drop down on the first note and spring up lightly on the second.

Flutter like a moth

leggiero

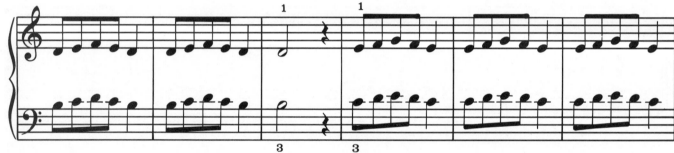

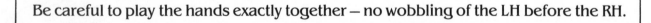

Be careful to play the hands exactly together — no wobbling of the LH before the RH.

14

Pounce like a cat on a mouse

Prepare the final chord during the rests in bar 7.

15

Hang upside down like a bat

Hold the first beat down; staccato on all others.

Hug like a bear

Cling to all notes.

16

Chirp like a cricket

Very short accented staccato notes.

Twitter like a blackbird

Strong accents.

Buzz like a bee

This is one octave!

For tone colour.

Drone like a wasp

Legato, thumb under.

18

Jump like a kangaroo

For accuracy, jump around in the rests.

Swoop like an eagle

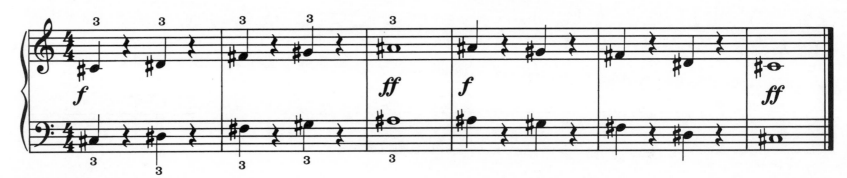

Dive-bomb with confidence on the black notes — don't worry if you slip off at first.
Play hands separately, then together.

Waddle like a penguin

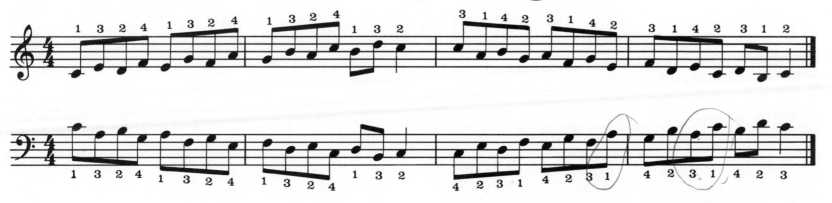

Learn the finger pattern – practise first on a table!

Kittens at play

Smooth take-overs between the hands.

Sprint like a greyhound

Practise slowly at first, speed up gradually.

The Waterman/Harewood Piano Series

	YOUNG BEGINNER		OLDER BEGINNER	INTERMEDIATE	ADVANCED
TUTORS	Me and My Piano 1	Me and My Piano 2	Piano Lessons 1	Piano Lessons 2	Piano Lessons 3
REPERTOIRE	Piano Playtime 1		Piano Playtime 2		
			Piano Progress 1		
			Piano Progress 2		
			Piano for Pleasure 1		
			Piano for Pleasure 2		
			The Young Pianist's Repertoire 1		
				The Young Pianist's Repertoire 2	
					Recital Repertoire 1
					Recital Repertoire 2
STUDIES		Piano Playtime Studies			
			Piano Progress Studies 1	Piano Progress Studies 2	
EXERCISES		Animal Magic			
THEORY	Monkey Puzzles 1	Monkey Puzzles 2			
MISCELLANEOUS		Nursery Rhyme Time			
		Christmas Carol Time			
			Merry Christmas Carols		
			Two at the Piano (duets)		
			The Secret (6 hands)		